REBEL GIRLS

Little Library

10 Women who Make Movies

This is a work of creative nonfiction. It is a collection of heartwarming and thought-provoking stories inspired by the lives and adventures of influential women. It is not an encyclopedic account of the events and accomplishments of their lives.

www.rebelgirls.com

Rebel Girls, Inc.
421 Elm Ave.
Larkspur, CA 94939

Text by Dinah Dunn
Art direction by Giulia Flamini
Graphic design by Kristen Brittain
Graphic design and additional illustrations: Alessandro Raimondo
Portrait illustrations: 4: Helen Li, 8: Marta Signori,
12: Adesewa Adekoya, 16: Palesa Monaren, 20: Monica Ahanonu,
24: Keisha Okafor, 28: Jeanetta Gonzales, 32: Taina Layla Cunion,
36: Marta Signori, 40:w Tyler Mishá Barnett

Printed in China, 2023
10 9 8 7 6 5 4 3 2 1
ISBN: 979-8-88964-075-2

FSC
www.fsc.org
MIX
Paper | Supporting responsible forestry
FSC™ C018179

CONTENTS

Alice Guy-Blaché

Filmmaker

July 1, 1873–March 24, 1968 | France and USA

Alice traveled all over the world as a child. She went from her grandmother's house in Switzerland to her mother's in France to her father's in Chile. All of those adventures made her brave.

When she grew up, Alice began working for a company that sold movie cameras. At the time, movies were new. To show how the camera worked, the company made short films of people doing normal things.

Alice knew she could do better. She had an idea. She asked her boss if she could make more interesting films. "It seems like a silly, girlish thing to do," he said. But if she finished all of her work for him first, he agreed she could do it.

In 1896, Alice created her first movie, *The Cabbage Fairy*. The film was only about one minute long. But it had costumes, a set, and a story. Her boss was pleased! Soon she was in charge of all the filmmaking.

As one of the first filmmakers, Alice had to figure out things on her own. Luckily, she had a great imagination. Movies at the time were in black and white. Alice added color by painting the film. She also figured out how to film along with a record playing, so the music matched the action. No one had ever done that before!

Alice moved to America. In 1910, she opened her own film studio. It became the largest in the country. Over the next 10 years, she made 1,000 films. She had hundreds of actors and directors working for her. She even had animals for her movies—including a 600-pound tiger named Princess!

By 1920, moviemaking became more expensive. Alice made her very last film. She could no longer afford to compete with the bigger studios. But she had already made her mark on the film world.

SCAN TO HEAR MORE!

Audrey Hepburn

Actor and Humanitarian

May 4, 1929–January 20, 1993 | Belgium, the Netherlands, and UK

Once upon a time, there was a little girl named Audrey who ate tulips. It wasn't because she loved flowers. She was just so hungry. Life was hard in the Netherlands during World War II. There was never enough food to go around. Audrey's empty stomach hurt. The tulip bulbs did not taste good, but they kept her from starving.

When Audrey grew up, she moved to England. First she became a model. Then she became an actor. She was good at it. After only a few years, she won an Academy Award—the greatest honor for an actor!

Soon Audrey was known all over the world for her talent and beauty. Fashion designers dressed her in beautiful clothes. She became known for her style.

Audrey's most famous film was *Breakfast at Tiffany's*. Women wanted to dress like her character. They wore her little black dress, long gloves, and diamond crown. They even visited the famous jewelry store in New York City where the movie was made.

But Audrey wanted to do more. She wanted to help others, especially poor and hungry children. She remembered how it felt!

Audrey started working with UNICEF. It was a charity that helped children around the world. It had even helped her when she was a girl. She believed that no child should ever be so hungry that they have to eat flowers.

Audrey traveled all over the world raising money for UNICEF. She spoke in front of Congress about the needs of children. For her work, she was awarded a Presidential Medal of Freedom. And when she died, a new white tulip was named after her.

Ava DuVernay

Filmmaker

Born August 24, 1972 | USA

Ava loved to make up stories. She and her sisters used their dolls to act out tales they dreamed up. But she never dreamed where it would take her.

After college, Ava got a job at a movie studio. She worked in the publicity department, which helped spread the news about movies coming out. There she learned the importance of telling stories that matter.

People of color were making great movies. But Ava noticed that these films didn't get as much attention. So she launched her own publicity company. She worked to make more people aware of Black, Latinx, Native American, and women filmmakers.

Then she started writing her own movies too.

Ava was 32 years old when she picked up a camera for the first time. She didn't have any experience directing, but that didn't stop her. She was a fast learner. Within a few years, Ava released her first movie!

Soon everyone knew her name. She directed dozens of films and TV shows. Many were about the history of Black people in America. Ava won awards for her movies. She also became the first Black woman to direct a film that cost more than $100 million to make.

Ava is now the head of her own film company. She uses it to work with young women and people of color who have interesting stories to tell. She said, “I will be there for whoever’s next.”

SCAN TO HEAR MORE!

Brenda Chapman

Director and Story Artist

Born November 1, 1962 | USA

Once there was a girl who began drawing as soon as she could hold a pencil. The red-haired girl's name was Brenda.

When she was 15 years old, Brenda called up Walt Disney Studios. *I'm really good at drawing*, she said. *Will you give me a job?* She was hopeful, but they told her no. *Try again when you learn more*, they said.

That's exactly what she did. She studied animation at an art school. There she made some short animated movies. One helped her get her dream job: working on animated films for Disney! She worked on many award-winning films, like *Beauty and the Beast* and *The Lion King*.

But she was one of the few women animators in the business. *Is that why the princesses in the movies always seemed so powerless?* she wondered. She decided to create a new type of princess: strong, smart, and . . .

. . . *Brave*, she thought. *What a great name for a film!*

Red-haired Princess Merida in *Brave* is anything but helpless. She shoots arrows and gallops on her horse. She fights off bears and has amazing adventures. Brenda based the character on her own daughter, Emma—a strong, free-spirited girl.

Not everyone believed in her story. It was so different from other movies!

People tried to get her to change the character to make her like other princesses. But Brenda stood her ground. And good thing she did! *Brave* went on to win an Academy Award and a Golden Globe.

When little girls watched the movie, they knew they could be like Merida. They could also be as strong, smart, and brave as the woman who made the movie.

Lupita Nyong'o

Actor

Born March 1, 1983 | Mexico, Kenya, and USA

Lupita wanted to grow up to be like her cool aunt. Amondi Buyu was wild and brave. She would shave her head and try odd hairstyles. She put on plays with the kids in the family. "She gave me courage to be daring," said Lupita.

Lupita's aunt also helped her try acting as a teenager. Lupita was afraid to make it her career. But she remembered her aunt's advice. Lupita decided to be brave. She went to college for acting.

Once she decided to act, success came fast. Lupita's first year out of college, she won an Academy Award! Lupita went on to act in plays and other award-winning movies.

Lupita used her interesting life to help her become the characters. She was born in Mexico and grew up in Kenya. Lupita then went by herself to America to go to college. She now speaks four languages: Luo, Spanish, English, and Swahili.

One day, Lupita was asked to be in the Marvel movie *Black Panther*. She was excited. *A film with Black superheroes?* she thought. *I would have loved this as a little girl!* She got the role of Nakia, a spy who helps people in need.

Lupita helps people in real life too. She works with Mother Health International to support poor women and children in places with wars or natural disasters. She enjoys her work with them. "We are using our power to lift each other up," she says.

Lupita is also known for her beauty. But her looks were hard for her to accept. She wrote a children's book about it. In it, a young Kenyan girl named Sulwe has the darkest skin in her family. Like Lupita, Sulwe learns to accept herself for who she is.

Actor and Executive Producer

Born August 14, 2004 | USA

Once there was a girl named Marsai who dreamed of becoming a superstar. When people asked her what she wanted to be when she grew up, she would say, "A legend!"

Marsai was an only child. She loved to put on performances in her family's living room. Her grandmother would watch movies with her. *Oh, Marsai could do that*, she'd say. Soon, Marsai believed it. When she was only five years old, she did her first commercial. It played on TVs all over Texas.

In 2013, her family moved to Los Angeles. They wanted to see if she could succeed at acting. A few months later, she made another commercial. But this one would be seen throughout the United States.

When she was nine years old, Marsai tried out for the role of Diane on the TV show *Black-ish*. She got the part! When the show came out, it was a huge hit. Her favorite part about playing Diane for years is getting to grow up with the character. She also grew close with the cast. "They're my second family," she said. The role made Marsai famous!

Marsai didn't just want to star in TV shows and movies—she wanted to make them too. So she started a company with her parents called Genius Productions. She had an idea for a movie with a cast of all

Black women. It was called *Little*. She presented the idea to movie companies. They loved it!

Marsai starred in the movie. She was also the executive producer. That meant she oversaw everyone's work on the movie. At just 13 years old, she was the youngest executive producer in Hollywood history. *Little* was a big success. Marsai's childhood wish came true—she has become a real-life legend.

Ruth E. Carter

Costume Designer

Born April 10, 1960 | USA

With drawings, fabric, and a sewing machine, Ruth helps create new worlds. She has made costumes for all kinds of characters.

How she dressed them helped show who they were. Some wore suits and shiny shoes. Some wore T-shirts and sneakers. Some wore glittering dresses. Some wore her most famous costume of all: a sleek black uniform with cat ears and claws.

It all began when she was a kid. Ruth's mother sent her to an after-school art program. There Ruth learned about African dances, drumming, poetry, and music. She was inspired. She started drawing her own clothing designs.

After college, she created costumes for plays. She also took care of the fancy clothes. Once, she looked out from backstage to see her mother standing there.

"You went four years to college to do laundry?" her mother asked.

"I'm still on my path, Mom," Ruth replied, trying not to roll her eyes.

Ruth's job was nothing like doing laundry. She read the movie scripts carefully. She searched through history for the right look. She chose colors and patterns that fit each film. Ruth worked on many movies and TV shows. She was nominated for two Academy Awards, but she didn't win.

For the movie *Black Panther*, she studied the fashion of African tribes, like the Xhosa, Zulu, Himba, and Maasai. She kept four words in mind for the design: beautiful, positive, forward, and colorful. She was again nominated for an Academy Award.

At the Oscars that year, Ruth sat in the audience. She felt excited and nervous. She knew *Black Panther* was some of her best work. Would she win this time?

And the Academy Award goes to . . . Ruth Carter! the presenter said.

Ruth jumped up from her seat. Everyone clapped and cheered. Ruth became the first Black costume designer to win an Academy Award.

Gymnast and Stuntwoman

Born November 18, 1993 | USA

Once upon a time, a two-year-old girl learned to do a cartwheel. She didn't know that this skill would one day land her in Hollywood.

Day after day in the gym, Sadiqua practiced flipping on the mat. She leapt on the balance beam. She swung on the uneven bars. By the time she turned 15, she was so good at gymnastics that she was coaching other kids.

In college, Sadiqua performed gymnastics routines to pop songs with a bright smile and feet covered in chalk. Her blue uniform sparkled as she soared through the air. Crowds clapped to the beat. They couldn't wait to see what she would do next.

When she graduated, Sadiqua was one of the best gymnasts in the country. She was famous for her double backflips. But Sadiqua's bravest leap was becoming one of Hollywood's youngest stuntpeople.

When a character in a movie has to do an action scene, sometimes a stuntperson takes over. And sometimes that person is Sadiqua. She trained to do the dangerous actions in movies. She might ride horses, jump motorcycles, or perform fight scenes.

It's not as easy as she makes it look on the big screen. It takes a lot of practice, and sometimes she gets hurt. But the job is exciting. Sadiqua always gets to try new things.

One day, she hopes to learn to drive planes and boats. Whether it's in the sky, on the water, or in a gym, Sadiqua can be found flipping fearlessly—just like she did when she was two.

SCAN TO HEAR MORE!

Sophia Loren

Actor

Born September 20, 1934 | Italy

Sophia's nickname as a child was Toothpick. She grew up in Naples, Italy, during World War II. She lived in a small apartment with her mom, her sister, her grandparents, and her aunt and uncle. Nobody ever had enough to eat.

Sophia's mom had dreamed of becoming an actor. When she heard that a director needed people to be in a movie in Rome, she went. She took Sophia with her. Sophia realized she liked being on set. She was just a teenager, but she decided to stay in Rome and try to become an actor.

Soon, Sophia turned into a beautiful young woman. She worked as a fashion model while she tried to break into movies.

Directors first noticed her looks. But they quickly found out that Sophia was also a talented actor. She became the most famous actor in Italy. Comedies, dramas, thrillers—she starred in them all.

At the time, Academy Awards were only given to actors who made movies in English. But Sophia was so good that she was nominated for an Academy Award for the Italian film *Two Women*. And she won! It was the first time an actor won for a performance in another language.

Hollywood also noticed Sophia's talent. Before long, American producers wanted to sign her to their next big film. She was nervous to act in English. But she decided to be brave and was soon just as successful in America.

"If you have fear, you have to conquer it," Sophia once said. "Anything that you want in life. Anything, not just acting. If you're stubborn enough, one day you will get it." And Sophia did.

Zendaya

Actor and Singer

Born September 1, 1996 | USA

Once upon a time in the city of Oakland, California, there was a shy girl who rarely spoke. Zendaya was so afraid to talk during class that she had to repeat kindergarten. But when she went with her mom to her job at a local theater, things changed.

Every night, Zendaya would eat dinner backstage with the actors. She would then set up a cozy spot with pillows and blankets in the back of the theater. She loved everything about the show: the lights, the costumes, the music.

Soon Zendaya was taking theater classes and performing too. As she grew up, Zendaya acted in TV and movies. When she was 14 years old, she played the dancer Rocky Blue

in the Disney show *Shake It Up!* She played a trapeze artist flying through the air in *The Greatest Showman*. She was even cast as Spider-Man's best friend! At 24 years old, Zendaya became the youngest actor ever to win an Emmy Award as a lead actress in a drama.

The girl who was too shy to say a word in kindergarten now enjoys the spotlight. And she loves playing with fashion. She once went to an event wearing a light-blue, light-up Cinderella ball gown. She even carried a glittery pumpkin carriage purse. People couldn't look away!

Zendaya uses her voice to address important issues, such as race in Hollywood. She speaks up when actors with darker skin aren't treated fairly. "I want to be a part of the change," she says.

About Rebel Girls

Rebel Girls is a global, multi-platform empowerment brand dedicated to helping raise the most inspired and confident generation of girls through content, experiences, products, and community. Originating from an international best-selling children's book, Rebel Girls amplifies stories of real-life women throughout history, geography, and field of excellence. With a growing community of nearly 20 million self-identified Rebel Girls spanning more than 100 countries, the brand engages with Generation Alpha through its book series, award-winning podcast, events, and merchandise. With the 2021 launch of the Rebel Girls app, the company has created a flagship destination for girls to explore a wondrous world filled with inspiring true stories of extraordinary women.

As a B Corp, we're part of a global community of businesses that meet high standards of social and environmental impact.

Join the Rebel Girls community:

Facebook: facebook.com/rebelgirls
Instagram: @rebelgirls
Twitter: @rebelgirlsbook
TikTok: @rebelgirlsbook
Web: rebelgirls.com
Podcast: rebelgirls.com/podcast
App: rebelgirls.com/audio

If you liked this book, please take a moment to review it wherever you prefer!